Whatever you can do or dream, you can, begin it. Boldness has genius, power and magic in it.

— Goethe —

BEYOND THE RABBIT HOLE

WRITING MY WAY TO TOMORROW

Judy
! Thanks for a lifetime of
friendship. For being there always
for loving me and believing in
me   Love BJ.

EJ SWANSON

FriesenPress

One Printers Way
Altona, MB R0G 0B0
Canada

www.friesenpress.com

ISBN
978-1-03-913534-5 (Hardcover)
978-1-03-913533-8 (Paperback)
978-1-03-913535-2 (eBook)

1. POETRY, CANADIAN

Distributed to the trade by The Ingram Book Company

TO THE FAM

TABLE OF CONTENTS

ACKNOWLEDGMENTS

To my Beta Buddies, Anne, Babs, and Judy, thank you for believing that I could do this, for propping up a sagging ego on occasion and for ever-thoughtful comments. I needed all of you on this journey.

And to my darling James, who saves me every day from myself, thank you for listening to poetry, for trying yoga and encouraging me to "be a mountain."

FOREWORD

Months after retiring from a thirty-year-plus practice of law I had a small breakdown followed by a breakthrough. The crisis brought me face to face with the question of *who am I now*? The *now* meaning now that I no longer work, now that I am officially a senior now that I no longer make a difference. My post-retirement life had been full up to that point with superficial but important things like selling homes and buying homes, moving, establishing new roots, and dealing with health issues. Suddenly, all that busy-ness was behind me, and I felt empty and without purpose. I decided to give myself time to grieve the life that I had moved on from. I had so badly underestimated the impact of that loss and so greatly overestimated my ability to handle it. Then, I firmly told myself I would move forward.

Moving forward meant being honest, at least with myself, about who I was in the *now*. What was I passionate about? What did I find meaningful and fun and worthwhile? Looking for tools to help with this exploration of self, I discovered mindful meditation and the teachings of Jon Kabat-Zinn, the author of *Full Catastrophe Living*. Practising meditation, even as a novice, took me inside myself in a safe and meaningful way. I felt free to take a look at my past experiences and the *me* I had been at various points in my life. I whispered the question *who are you now?* Among the answers whispered back was *you are a writer.*

An avid reader as a child, I found early on that I loved to write too. I excelled at writing throughout my school days, through university, and eventually made a career of it. The practice of law relies heavily on clear communication, both verbal and written, and I was good at it. Alongside law I wrote skits and stories, plays and lyrics for fun and for sharing with friends and family. I was acknowledged as someone who wrote well but not as a *writer* per se.

All these years later I revisited past writings and was encouraged. *Not too bad*, I thought. I began to write daily. *Beyond the Rabbit Hole* is the result of revisiting earlier works and more recent writing. It is a collection of poetry, stories, and reflections that describe where I have been, where I am now, and, occasionally, my vision of the future. While it is short enough to read cover-to-cover at one go, my hope is that it becomes the type of book kept by your bed or on a table somewhere so that it can be read slowly or over and over again. If it makes you think, if it touches your heart, if it makes you laugh out loud, I will be content.

POETRY

BITS AND PIECES

Just one breath and then another
I go inside myself and there discover
Bits and pieces of my life.

Some lived, some dreamed
The unremembered and the unseen
Yet live again inside of me.

Surely the I of me can be gentle
As pieces of remembrance settle
Into the now of my existence.

The rise and fall of every breath
Reveals to me my deep regret
For things done and not done still.

Am I healed then? Am I whole?
If I take into eternal soul these
Parts of me to live again?

No longer good, no longer bad
Just bits of life that I once had
That rise again with just one breath

And then another.

CHILD

Go back for the child you left behind
Frightened and weeping under the tree
Look over your shoulder now
And you will see her.

Go back for the child you left alone
To live the terror of uncertainty and anger
While you tried to outrun
Your own fear.

You were not strong then when you ran
And could not carry the burden of the child.
Now in your old age you are strong
You can heal her.

Do you see her? I do.
Will you go back for her? I will.
Can you heal her? I can.
And do you love her? How can I not?

She is inside me waiting.

SHIP OF DREAMS

You can sail with anyone
Or no one at all
All baggage must be left behind
What you need is waiting
On the Ship of Dreams

You can go anywhere you desire
Or sit absolutely still
Destinations are optional
The journey is everything
On the Ship of Dreams

You are the Captain, the Crew, and Passenger
Choices are yours to make
Imagination and desire set the course
Courage and hope fill the sails
On the Ship of Dreams

Those who would doubt or judge you
Are left behind on the shore
What you do, where you go, who you are
Is shaped by possibility and whimsy
On the Ship of Dreams

Last night I sailed the Ship of Dreams
With you beside me
We watched the stars and wondered
About everything and nothing
Pain and age did not sail with us
On the Ship of Dreams

Will you come with me again
On the Ship of Dreams?

6 AM AT THE LAKE HOUSE

It is already hot in the sun
As I sit on my porch drinking
My first cup of coffee.

I move my chair to find shade
From which I can observe
The lake in the new day.

No wind yet, so the water
Has only small ripples
And glistens with reflected heat.

Across the lake are rolling hills
In vibrant shades of green while above
A cloudless sky watches and waits.

Only the sound of water, trees
Moving with the slight breeze, and
Birds, though even they speak softly.

The heat of the sun dominates all.
Me with my coffee, the movement
Of water, trees, and the birds.

It will be a coping day. A day to
Draw blinds and turn on fans
Plan salads for supper.

Soon the sounds of people will
Break this early morning time
As they too take stock of the day.

The lake is still cold but bearable
For the young and the hardy
A place to soften the heat with cool water.

Coffee done, I get up and get on
With busy life things so that nothing needs
Doing once the true heat arrives.

I may swim today. Shiver by shiver
Gather courage to dive in, and then
I will laugh, triumphant and whole.

This will become my memory
Of this hot June day. Laughing
In cold water in the heat of the sun.

OUT OF TIME

Let me give you this memory.
You are standing along the railing
On an upper deck of a cruise ship
Somewhere in the Caribbean Sea.

It is nighttime and almost no one
Is around. The sea is calm, although
A light breeze lifts your hair off
Of your neck and ruffles your dress.

You can hear dance music
Playing somewhere on the ship
But not so close as to disturb
Your aloneness.

You look out across the flat ocean
And you can see to the very
Ends of the earth. And then
You look up into the sky.

And—oh—the stars take your
Breath away. They are so
Different here in the middle of
Darkness, in the middle of the sea.

They are bigger and brighter and
You can actually see patterns
Although you do not know
The names of constellations.

Your awareness of self fades away
And you become part of the darkness,
Part of the expanse of the water,
Part of the universe of the sky.

Time stops as you experience
Not having a separate existence.
Feeling instead what it is like
To be part of the all, the whole.

How long you stand this way
Feeling this way is hard to measure.
At some point though you come
Back to yourself.

Back to yourself, at the railing
On a cruise ship, in the darkness
Sailing the Caribbean
Living a memory.

THINK ABOUT IT

As for those who choose to believe
They are not uniformly naive
For what all cynics miss
Is most certainly this
Facts often start out as a dream

AM I TOO OLD?

I am not done yet
But I keep getting older
And it's starting to feel
Like I am running out
Of time. I need more
Time to improve myself.
To speak Spanish better,
To do yoga every day,
To learn to dance again.
I need more time to watch
My granddaughters grow
Into women and my sons
And daughter turn into
Middle-aged adults.
I need more time to
Love the gentle man
Who is my husband.
I need more time
For laughter, more
Time to look at paintings.
I need more time to become
Wise and then maybe
I will understand that
One can never be too old
For life to happen.

AND I REPLY

Every morning my husband asks
How I am, and I understand
That he is wondering about
Pain, and whether I will
Be living the day at a
Distance, distracted by it.
I summon my better angels
And say, *Not too bad.*
Better than yesterday, maybe.
Sometimes this is true.

I read an email from a friend.
She, too, begins with a
How are you? Then goes
On to tell me about her life.
I know that at some level
She really wants to know
How I am. Just maybe
Not in detail. Or right now.
I ignore the question and
Focus on what she has to say.

The cashier at the local grocery,
The delivery man with a parcel,
The neighbour next door,
All want to know how I am.
They really mean *How is your day?*
How is life? And I answer,
I'm great, as though
It mattered or they were listening.
It doesn't, though, and they
Usually aren't.

Such a simple question, really:
How are you? But I am
Tired of thinking about
How I am because Pain and
Fatigue have such loud voices.
It is easy to forget that
There are bright and happy
Moments in my life that need
To be celebrated. *It's*
Complicated, I think, and
Perhaps that is the best
Answer of all.

DANCING

It's late afternoon and she is sitting in her favourite chair.
Eyes closed, head back, hands gently folded in her lap.
Watchers would say that she is resting or even asleep.
They would be mistaken, though.

She has instead gone inside herself, reserving energy,
Prolonging her ability to cope with what is there.
If it is a good day, to even rise above it
Prayerfully and playfully.

It has been a long day and will be a longer night.
The pills aren't working; she could take more.
Conceding defeat as sometimes happens,
For even the brave and the strong must rest.

Instead, she asks Google to play music from the 70s
And as a favourite song begins, she rises stiffly,
Standing there swaying slightly side to side, arms rising
Gracefully alongside her head.

She moves one foot, taking a step, and then moves
The other so that she enters into open space
And begins to move in time with the music,
Ignoring complaints from within.

She closes her eyes and smiles as her arms
Embrace an unseen partner seductively.
And with tears trickling down aging cheeks
She dances with Pain.

BREATHING IN RAINBOWS

The ancient ones assigned
Colours to the seven chakras like this:
Red, orange, yellow, green
Blue, indigo, and violet.
A coincidence that these
Are the colours of the rainbow?
Did an ancient one breathe
In a rainbow one day?
How delightful symmetry is!

MEDITATION ON THE FIRST CHAKRA

Not lost. Found.
Not lost. Found.
I am not lost; I am found.
I was lost then; I am found now.
In the now, in this moment, I am
Strong and grounded in my life.
The loneliness and sadness of then
Has no place in the now, and so
It is gone. Not hidden but gone.
Strength has washed it away.
I am here in the now, fully
Awake and aware of being
Myself, complete and perfect
Just as I am in this moment.
Found. Not lost.
Found. Not lost.

MOUNTAIN

It sits just being itself.
Needing nothing, it
Offers much by simply
Existing.
There is no time,
Or if there is time,
Then the Mountain
Is outside of it.
It changes without
Needing to, accepting
Change for what it
Is. Just change.
Neither happy nor sad,
The Mountain, beyond
Its own existence,
Is content.
As I sit contemplating
Being that Mountain
I too need nothing, feel
Nothing, not even pain.
I am simply content
In the now of this moment
To be whole and complete
As I am. A mountain.
With the strength and
Wisdom to go on. Just
Being what I am. And
For now, that is enough.

MEDITATION 101

As I sink into my body,
Grounded by the physical,
Another me floats untethered
On insubstantial air.
Bliss.

AND SO...

If wisdom is recognizing
Things as they truly are,
Tell me, wise ones,
Is the glass half empty
Or is the glass half full?

THE WISE ONES REPLY

Show us this glass, they say,
So that we might see it.
I bring them the glass
Of water that I have
Wondered about because
I don't know if it is
Half empty or half full.

They behold the glass and
Say: It is both, it is neither,
It is simply a glass that
Contains water. It does not
Care whether it is half empty
Or if it is half full, why
Should you?

I say, I need to know
If I should be happy or sad
About the amount of water
In the glass. The Wise Ones
Laugh. Be one or neither,
The amount of water will
Be the same.

OUT OF BODY

I am meditating, checking in
With all parts of my body
Breathing into my toes, then,
On an out breath, letting
My toes dissolve from awareness.

Soon I am without toes,
Feet, ankles, and legs.
Once visited and experienced
They too dissolve and are
Banished from awareness.

I travel on air. I ride
Each breath as it moves
In and out of my body lifting
My belly, then as I let that go
My chest, in time with my heart.

Torso gone, chest gone, neck gone.
Now I breathe with my face as
I move into my cranium where
I imagine my mind lives. Then
That too dissolves.

I have run out of body. It has vanished.
All that remains of me
Is air as I experience existence
As breath.

FLIGHT

Airborne, I become intensely loyal to the ground
And anxiously await to become earthbound
Again.

(MY) ODE TO JOY

When joy unfurls its mighty wings
And carries us to lofty heights
It causes every heart to sing
Of justice, beauty, glorious sights
Elation makes bright visions of
The life we're given each to live
To search for wisdom, peace, and love
For others, strength and joy to give
Let in full gladness and belief
In better times that are to come
The bless'd surrender to relief
All past sorrows now undone
As to joy we give our hearts
New, sweeter secrets to impart

THE BEHOLDER

She sees it in the face of a child
Or in the opening of a flower
She may glimpse it watching
A group of old men playing
Chess and laughing or
In the weathered exterior of
An old house. She is not
Looking for perfection. Instead
She is looking for that elusive
Something that is interesting,
Beautiful, alive. And because
She can see it, she can capture
It with her camera so that
Others can see what she
Does. Her gift is in the
Seeing. She is a Beholder
And when she shares
Her vision, we look through
Her eyes at the magic
She has found.

EJ SWANSON

NO WORDS

Nothing in writing, you said.
Not one word.
So instead, I send you
Not one word but many.
Not nothing but everything.

YOUNG WOMAN'S LAMENT

Isn't it a lovely day—look at that sunshine!
Couldn't you just stay with me and
While away the time?
Why is it you must leave me?
Why is it you must go?
Is it something that I said?
I'd really like to know.

Those things you said to me last night
Couldn't have been true. Does the morning
Alter us or just the things we do?
Have I changed completely now
You've seen me in the light? Then
Honey we weren't making love
Like you swore to me last night.

If you could just stay a while
Maybe have a cup of tea
I'd have a moment to recall
Where I left my dignity.
Did it come off with all my clothes?
I hope that wasn't so
But if you really have to leave
I guess I'll never know.

EJ SWANSON

Don't ask me for my number
I know that you won't call
Why do men say the same damn
Thing meaning nothing after all
I'd rather that you left me
With empty promises unsaid
It hurts enough to realize
That I have been misled.

Oh, woman sings a love song
The man walks out the door
And so she grieves another loss
Not the one she's looking for
Not the love she's longing for
Not the life she's waiting for
But tonight is one night more.

YOU AGAIN

The love between you and me
Is ancient and ended long ago.
Why then do I feel it now?

I see you sitting watching
The pale moon rise over still water
And, taking your hand in mine, say nothing.

If I listen, I can hear your heart beating
An echo of another time and place
While this life and this love

Begin again.

PUPPET MASTER

First, may I congratulate you
On your unconscious devotion
To manipulation? As it takes
Two to compete the act I
Choose not to dance when you
Pull my strings, leaving you
Blameless.

I wish though that our
Relationship could be altered
So that I might be my
True self with you and
You with me, instead of you
Needing to be in total
Control.

That is not likely to happen though,
Given our age, our history, and
Our circumstances. But I cannot
Regret what I cannot change.
So I have taken the liberty of
Cutting the strings, setting us both
Free.

SCAR TISSUE

Some things, once said,
Cannot be unsaid or,
Once heard, be unheard.
Words that cause pain
Leave wounds that
Must heal, leaving
Scars in their place.
I cannot unhear our
Last conversation, nor
Can I stop the hurt
Caused by the echo
Of your words.
You say your words were
Kindly meant, that you
Would never hurt me.
Funny then, that it
Happens so often. Still
I suppose I will forgive
What I cannot unhear
Lest the fragile truce of
Friendship be undone.

SAVING JUDY

The first time I saved Judy
I took her out for air because
She felt faint at a meeting.
We sat on swings, breathing.
Then she said, *I'm pregnant,*
And burst into tears.
She was newly married and
When she'd told him her news
Her husband looked at her
And went out to shovel snow.
Husbands are like that, I told her.
They need time to adjust.
Look at Joseph, I said,
Even with the Christ Child
On the way he needed
Convincing. We laughed
And became friends.
The second time I saved Judy
She had four children and
Her husband was barely
Alive, injured beyond repair.
Stay close to me, she said.
Don't leave me.
I flew with her to where
Her husband lay dying and
Stayed with her while
She kissed him and said
Goodbye. I sang at his
Funeral and after it was

Over, we cried.
The third time I saved Judy
She was camping on
A beach in Mexico, washing
Clothes in an old suitcase
That had been swept onshore.
I need you to come down,
She said. *This is hard.*
We went, my family and I,
To where she was with her
Family and together we
Made memories that make
Us laugh to this day.
And thus it has been for
More than forty years of
Friendship. We have
Shared so much, made
So many memories that
We are now soul kin.
I am her son's godmother;
She is godmother to mine.
We can open each other's
Refrigerators and look inside.
We open closets without fear.
We already know about
The skeletons.
When we were young, we
Said to each other, *When*
We are old women we

Will sit together on a
Front step somewhere
With grandchildren on
Our knees. We did that
The other day, and smiled
Remembering our younger
Selves. Saving Judy
Was what I did because
She and I were friends.
And because we were friends
Judy saved me right back.
I suspect that we will go on
Saving each other until
We say goodbye, for now.
Smiling because we know
That we will meet again.

PLEASE LISTEN

I need to know how to express
My rage more quietly
So that you will understand
That what I have to say is important
Enough to live through my anger.

SIX WEEKS

Six weeks ago, just six
We sat under the Mexican sun wondering
If we should maybe go home early
We sipped drinks and went for a swim
Thought about going to town to shop
Still making plans for the future

Six weeks ago we hugged friends
Elbows bumping hello on occasion
Maskless, we isolated by choice
Not because we had to, factoring
COVID into decisions, but vaguely
Like the needs of a stranger

Suddenly airports were closing
The kids said please come home
So we went, wipes and masks
In hand to sit on a plane inches
Away from others, feeling
The irony of travelling to safety
In such a dangerous way

Then home to forced isolation
Waving to family from windows
Living a COVID existence
We wait for the latest statistics
Wondering if the world has
Run out of safe places to be

Out of quarantine we carefully
Go for solitary walks as numbers
Of cases and deaths keep rising
We shop online because going out
Means face masks and maybe close
Contact. We are afraid all the time now

The condo keeps getting smaller
But there is nowhere else to be
Stay home, we are told by doctors
Who are the new media stars
Businesses close, the economy flounders
Trump suggests that we inject disinfectant
Six weeks from now what will life be?
Will there be a vaccine?
Will we be able to see our family?
Will masks be a fashion statement?
Will there be a new world, a new normal?
Will I like it?

They say more waves are coming
Bringing new cases, more deaths.
We wait, wondering, staying home,
Staying apart, staying safe. While
We are all lonely and desperate,
Praying for this pandemic to end.

FIRE SEASON

Maybe it was the heat or
The lousy day at work. Maybe
The lack of sleep the night before.
Who knows exactly what
Set us off. I started it,
I know I did, but you were
Quick to respond as though
Waiting for a spark to
Ignite your anger. At me,
At all the (other) stupid people
Who had inserted themselves
Into your life today. And, unthinking,
Because I was tired and hot and
Miserable, I fed your rage with
My own. A firestorm of
Red words and incendiary accusations
About nothing that really mattered
Except at that moment and then only
As ammunition. Then you started to cry
And so did I. Hot tears of hurt and
Regret and incredulity. Where had
Those feelings, those words, come from?
Did I mean what I said? Did you?
Suddenly spent, unfuelled and empty
We took stock of the damage in
Silence. How bad was it? Could we
Recover from this? How long
Would it take? You reached for me
And together we swept away the ashes.

VALLEY OF THE SUN

The forests are burning in the
Valley of the Sun. This is
Where we live our summers
By a cold mountain lake in
A valley surrounded by
Green mountains. Only
This year the days have been
Too hot and even the lake
Is warm when we swim.
Months without rain and
The air is heavy,
Tasting of smoke and worry.
Wildfires burn out of control
Fed by the dry grasses of the hills.
Nothing stops the flames that are
Orange and red and streaked with
Smoke rising in the wind of the
Fire, then sinking to smother valleys.
It has been too hot this summer
An unnatural heat that shatters
Records. Some people say that
Rain will come soon and put out
The fire and purge the smoke.
I want to believe them—I do—
But as I watch the forests burn
I wonder if this time it is
Too late for rain.

THE LUCKY ONE

When I am with him
I sink gratefully into trust
Knowing that my well-being
Is first in his mind and intent.

The experience of being first,
Even over self, is powerful
So, in turn, his well-being must be
The object of my own intent.

We love in this way, each
Being first with the other,
Despite our egos which demand
Their turn in the sun.

There are misunderstandings
That sometimes lead to anger and
Cruel words—who knows better how
To craft a blow than your mate?

When they see him open my door,
Or lean over to kiss me, or reach
For my hand, other women say
You're a lucky one, aren't you?

And I always answer, yes
It is true that luck has led to
This love, but so has hard work
For if I am a lucky one, so is he.

PURPLE SUNSHINE

I bite into a just-picked
Blueberry
And it squirts summertime
Into my mouth.

ODE TO THE TUB

At weary end of dreary day
When all must-dos are past
It's such a lovely thing to say
I'm off to take a bath!

BLOWING BUBBLES

When our children were young
I would buy bubbles for them
To blow and chase around
The yard. We would see rainbows
In some and others would land
Like kisses on blades of grass.
Bubbles would burst on noses
And lips leaving the taste
Of soap behind. Some took
A ride on the wind, leaving
Us to watch a journey
We could only imagine.
Yesterday I had a bad day.
So many things to worry
About or do, or solve.
I bought bubbles and sat
In a park blowing all
Of these away. I looked
For rainbows instead, or
Soft landings on the lawn.
I felt the softest touch of
A wayward bubble landing
On my upturned face. I
Watched bubbles float
Away on the wind and
Imagined I was floating
Too. When my time comes,
As it inevitably will, please
Don't play hymns or recite

Poetry or even passages
From inspirational literature.
Bring me bubbles instead.
Together we can lift me up
To whatever heaven awaits.

YOU LOST ME AT INSECTS

There is much I admire
And would choose to adopt
About the practice of Buddhism.
For starters, I rather like
The thought of being awake,
Working towards enlightenment.
I had imagined being awake
Already, but now I understand
That it was the wrong sort of
Consciousness I had awoken to.
My consciousness involved duty
And work and so on. Instead
I need to set my sights on
Nothingness. I must strive to
Be patient, to give freely, and
To seek wisdom in all that I do.
I must practise these virtues
Diligently and meditate as well.
And all this I was prepared to do.
But then came the necessity
Of seeking the well-being of
All living things, including
Insects and snakes, and you lost me
There and then. I am simply
Not prepared to be kind to
Mosquitoes or wasps or anything
That slithers. Frankly, Buddhists,
You might want to rethink this one.

JUST FOR FUN

Three trees were standing
Around in the forest
Chatting amongst themselves.
Said one: I like it here. My top
Branches can see a long way—
Right to the mountains.
Said another: I like it here.
The wind is just right so that
I can wave hello to friends
In other parts of the forest.
Said the third: I like it here.
My roots are buried deep in
The woody soil and I can feel
Cold water far below.
Shall we stay then? They
Asked each other.
Why not? They answered.
It's not as if we had
Anywhere else to go.
So they stayed, firmly
Rooted to the spot.

REFLECTIONS AND
SHORT STORIES

A CALL TO ARMS

Yesterday I gave a stern talking to my arms, having been horrified by the amount of dangling skin underneath them. *Look at yourselves,* I said. *You are letting us down with all that excess baggage. You simply are not trying hard enough.* To emphasize my point, I gave my arms a good shake and then had to wait until the jiggling stopped.

They, the flabby bits that is, were not impressed. *What about you?* they demanded indignantly. *You're the one that created this situation,* they said. *Do you think that we* enjoy *looking like this?*

Surprised by this abrupt shift in blame, I was hard-pressed to come up with a response. *Well,* I answered hesitantly, *I suppose that I had something to do with it, perhaps let the old diet slip a bit and I haven't been swimming or doing weights lately either. Still,* I rallied, *surely you could exercise some restraint in fat production. Maybe pass some along to, say, the bustline?*

I think I heard the arms snort at this suggestion.

After this exchange, I knew that Destination Shapely Arms was going to be up to me. That the arms were not interested in independent action. After a few days of a lightweight workout I decided that an alternative might be to never go sleeveless. Operation Cover Up was put into action.

I have avoided further discussions with my arms, the first having been so unsatisfying. The other night in my bath, I did try addressing my stomach. I can't even begin to tell you what *it* had to say.

THE GLEANERS

He is roguishly handsome with his full mustache and open shirt, tired perhaps from a hot day in the field cutting wheat. She is buxom and lovely, obviously past her first bloom as the look in her eyes is knowing rather than innocent. He is looking at her adoringly; she is looking away demurely with lips turned up in the sort of smile a woman smiles when someone she loves finds her beautiful.

My mother called the two of them "The Gleaners," and as far back as I can remember the figurines had pride of place in our home. She would not be parted from them, even though they were in later years broken and only partially repaired. Mom dealt with the missing bits by knitting a serape for the Man that she flung jauntily over his shoulder covering the hole where his back once was. I seem to remember that the Woman, though obviously no longer whole, had all of her parts.

This is how the Gleaners came into my life and how they remained for the rest of my mother's. Rare and delicate porcelain figures whose very imperfection made them special and unique. In that way, the Gleaners reminded me of her.

Two events dramatically altered and then shaped my mother's life: her father died when she was nine years old, and when she was forty-two she became a paraplegic. Neither of these events were her fault, neither within her control.

By her own account and those of her contemporaries, Mom was a bright, attractive, outgoing, and mischievous child. She was dark-haired and slim with—and this was important—pretty feet. All of her life Mom had a glow about her, an energy that might be described by the word "radiance." You knew when she was in the room and when she was not. People were drawn to her, loved talking with her, and were comforted by her.

She could be demanding, impatient, autocratic, and catty. She had a unique style of backhanded insults. What started out as a compliment could, midstream, become something else entirely. For example: "That's a lovely outfit, dear. I didn't know that they had such things in your size." I was never sure such slips were unintentional.

Mom had one blue eye and one that was part hazel and part blue. On Mom, this looked exotic, not strange. She could carry off having two different coloured eyes in the same way that she could carry off wearing only one earring or having lipstick on her teeth.

My mother's father's name was Fred Patterson and she adored him. Through Mom's memories, I imagined a tall, handsome man who was sociable, caring, and successful. He spoke French fluently, a fact Mom took great pride in as a mark of distinction in the small Alberta town where she grew up. He loved animals and had a special way with them. And I suspect—though it was never said explicitly— that his second daughter, my mother, was his pet.

I think that when my mother's father died of a heart attack when she was ten, her own heart broke. She lost a hero, the person who made her feel safe and secure, the person who loved her best. Mom was not my grandmother's favourite child. That might have been her older sister or her younger brother, but it was definitely not her.

My grandmother came from Glasgow, Scotland nadwore picture hats and dress gloves. She was an accomplished pianist and singer with well-heeled friends with names like Jessie Short and Mrs. Jack. My grandmother liked the finer things of life and, while my grandfather was alive, had them given to her. The stories Mom told about Grandma Mac were often funny (like the time she drove the car into a haystack) or admiring (Grandma was very particular about her appearance and would never appear in public without her hat and gloves, even to play Pitch and Putt) but never tender. That makes sense to me, as I don't remember ever sitting on Grandma Mac's knee or being comforted or cosseted by her either.

When my grandfather died, things changed. There wasn't a lot of money. Grandma remarried a nice but ineffectual fellow by the name of Fraser MacDonald. Mom's older sister went off to teacher training with the promise that she would pay for Mom to take the same course, in her turn. That promise was not kept. Instead, her sister married almost right out of training. That broken promise haunted my mother the rest of her life.

This left my mother caught between what young ladies could and couldn't do. Young ladies of quality but little money could not, for example, work in a doctor's office. They could not become secretaries or nurses. They could become teachers, at least until they married, or they could stay quietly at home waiting for the right man to come along. In my mother's case she married my father—not the right man, as it turned out—because her mother liked him and my mother wanted out of her mother's house.

My father was tall and handsome but did not speak French fluently or otherwise. He worked in a grocery store and, though intelligent, was not ambitious. My father's father worked in a coal mine and his mother, potentially a woman of great character, retreated into a haze of cigarette smoke and arthritis. My father did not come from a background where tea was served in china cups so fine that you could almost see through them. I don't think that he could imagine such a life nor would he have felt at home there. Dad was bright and charming but alarmingly content to settle for what was within easy reach.

Into this marriage of opposites came the Gleaners—or, at least my sister and I thought they were a wedding present from someone on our mother's side, maybe Mrs. Jack or Jessie Short. Made from fine porcelain and hand-painted, the figurines have no hallmark so their provenance is open to speculation. They may have come from Belgium or France, or perhaps even Scotland, and were likely made sometime in the mid to late 1800s.

My mother and father moved a lot, from one small-town grocery business to another. The Gleaners went with them, town to town, mantel to mantel. During one such move they were broken. The "darn McLeod boys" did it, not on purpose, but because they were strong young men more suited to baseball than the handling of fine china. Mom kept the pieces in a box or maybe a drawer, and for many years that is where they stayed.

The other defining event of my mother's life, becoming a paraplegic, might have happened before or after the breaking of the Gleaners. That detail is lost to me now. I do have vivid memories of the morning my mother woke up and was unable to feel anything from the waist down. I remember going with my father to pick up a very old wooden wheelchair from someone and I remember my mother sobbing with fear when she was lifted into it. Her life and the life of our family changed that morning in ways that we will never completely understand.

The paralysis was the result of an infection caused by surgical packing that should have been removed at the end of a surgical procedure but wasn't. My mother complained of pain and fever after the surgery but the doctors, WWII vintage men, attributed her complaints to menopause. Untreated, the infection eventually ate through her spinal column. At the time, neither doctors nor the hospital admitted to the error.

I was four, nearly five, when this happened. I watched my mother deal with things that would have defeated a lesser person. I watched her deal with a restricted life, pain, and indignities. I watched her rise above all of that so that her paralysis became a banner and not a burden, at least that's what she wanted people to believe. Her family lived a different truth. While I *watched*, my sister *did*. She is nine years older than me, so at thirteen she became my mother's caregiver and my watchdog. My father, feeling sorry for himself, burdened with a crippled wife whom he had long since stopped loving, simply faded away.

He left for the first time when I was sixteen, returned to walk me down the aisle at eighteen, and then left for good a few years later. I want to say, and I do believe, that he was not a bad person, simply inadequate under the circumstances. My mother needed a successful and strong partner to mend the hole created by her father's death. My father was charmingly mediocre. My mother needed a husband to demand action when she complained after the surgery. My father found her a wheelchair and expected her to adjust.

It was my sister who glued the Gleaners together. In retrospect this makes sense, as she also held the family together during those first dark days of paralysis. She put the Gleaners back together and my mother covered the holes that remained with a knitted serape and her unique brand of chutzpah. They were restored to their rightful place on the mantel, and there they remained until very recently.

I was the one who took them in the end. It was after my mother had been gone for several years and after my father's funeral. My sister and I went back to the condo she had shared with our mother right up to her death, and there were the Gleaners on the mantel. It became impossible for me to leave them there, still broken, still with the serape covering up holes that should never have been. I needed to fix them or destroy them. And so, with my sister's understanding, I packed them up in a box for yet another journey.

What my sister understood was my anguish that our fine mother had to make do all of her life. Make do without a beloved father, make do without a higher education, make do without a strong partner to love and provide for her, make do with a body that others had broken through neglect and indifference. I couldn't change any of that. But I could get the Gleaners fixed.

For a while I did nothing with them, just left them in the box. I didn't really know where to start. It was my husband who found a ceramic artist and took the Gleaners to show her. She thought she could do the job, but it would take time and, of course, money.

The Gleaners were with her for six months. I called after four months and she told me that she was working on them. I called a month later and she firmly told me to be patient—that restoration was an art. I waited for her to call me and finally she did. She said they were beautiful and that she hoped that I would be pleased with what she had been able to do.

I picked them up on a bright Saturday morning in June and brought them home. So perfectly restored that it was impossible to tell that the Man had ever had a serape over his shoulder and not a scythe or that the Woman's face had had a crack running through it. I put them on my mantel, and I cried.

It has been several years now since I brought the Gleaners home. I've gotten used to how they look, and it takes longer each day to remember where the holes were. Even as I cherish their perfection, something is missing. I thought maybe that it was the serape that my mother knitted, but now, as I write this, it occurs to me that I am in fact missing her.

In making things do, she changed them and made them different, more alive. She did that with the Gleaners and she did that with her own life. Maybe she would have made a serape for the Man even if he had never been broken. Just to liven things up a little. I don't know for sure, but I wouldn't put it past her.

Broken things can be mended. Hurts can heal. Families can re-shape themselves. There is beauty in imperfection that deserves celebration when it is handled the right way. Like a serape over the shoulder of a priceless figurine, or a hat at a jaunty angle on the head of a woman with two different coloured eyes and one earring, sitting proudly in her electric cart, loving life.

GOD DAMNED GEORGE

I need to tell you about pain, as it has been my constant companion for more than thirty years. Chronic Pain, sometimes Big Pain, sometimes Quiet Pain. In unpacking my life, it has stared me right in the face, daring me to disclose it. Like a badly kept secret, those closest to me know all about it, and acquaintances might wonder what is wrong with me.

I have always thought about pain as an entity distinct from me. It is not *my* pain; it is rather *the* pain or just Pain. I decided to give a name to this pain. Its name is George and because I am not a fan, God Damned George.

God Damned George arrived about six months after the birth of my youngest son. I was thirty-three, happily married, and had an interesting practice in environmental law. My health was good, I thought. Apart from struggles with weight, I was strong, had lots of energy, and was rarely ill. Then I started to ache everywhere—literally everywhere—from the tips of my ears to individual toes. God Damned George announced his presence with a flourish, taking up residence boldly in my flesh.

Trying to describe him to my doctor was difficult. The best I could come up with was "I hurt. I hurt everywhere especially in my *meat*." What a symptom to present with. I was lucky, though, as my doctor was a gifted diagnostician. He gave me an article to read about a relatively new cluster of symptoms labelled *Fibromyalgia* and told me to come back when I had read it. I did, and we agreed that God Damned George was likely that. A chronic disorder, prevalent in Type A women, of pain, fatigue, cognitive impairment, and digestive issues. There is no known cause, no laboratory test to detect it, and no cure. Treatment included exercise, massage, and medication typically associated with depression.

Thirty-six years later, nothing much has changed with the original diagnosis or treatment and God Damned George has had a field day interfering with my life. I have tried everything from acupuncture to hypnosis to CBD oil. Sometimes God Damned George is confused and backs off a bit while he comes up with a strategy to combat the most recent remedy. He is canny and so inevitably comes roaring back, unfazed by my attempts to get rid of him. He now has allies that showed up as I got older. Joining him in his mission to rule my life are osteoarthritis and back pain. A demonic trio that tries to seduce me into a medicated fog while they have their way with my body. *Nice try, God Damned George. You and your buddies still have* me *to contend with.*

God Damned George is moody. Sometimes he is all feisty and hurls pain at me so that my mind is full of its noise. Other times he is depressed and confused and floods me with his emotions. Then there are the tired times when all he wants to do is sleep—usually after living it up by being feisty for several days in a row.

Because God Damned George is invisible, because there are no laboratory results to wave in front of people's noses, I sometimes feel like a sham, a charlatan who is feigning symptoms to get sympathy or to avoid physical activity. I am ashamed of being in the company of God Damned George and feel less of a person because of it. I feel sorry for my family when I cannot do something because I am too tired or too down or hurt too much. I will not give up though. God

Damned George may restrict my movements, make me so tired that all I can do is sleep, and cloud my mind, *but he will not rule my life.*

So, take that, God Damned George. And while you are at it, find somewhere else to go. I have things to do.

THE WOMAN IN MY CLOSETS

A woman has invaded my closets and she has far too many clothes. While her identity has not been confirmed, I feel like I must know her for the clothes look somewhat familiar.

I opened my closet at the Lake House for the first time this season and saw with dismay that she had arrived before me. My side of the closet was jam packed and hollered redundancy. Clearly that was the effect of dual occupancy for what else would explain the presence of eight pairs of black pants, fourteen stretchy jersey maxi dresses, and God knows how many white tops. Among the collection, I recognized old favourites of my own. Seldom worn but too precious to be gotten rid of, they occupied space by right if not utility.

The invasion of my closet at the Lake House is not a novel experience. The same woman has clothes in my closet in Mexico and in Sherwood Park. Some of her things are in poor shape and frankly in poor taste. What is the point, I wonder, in holding on to T-shirts stained beyond redemption or sweaters stretched out of shape? She clearly has trouble maintaining a steady weight, as some things are size ten and others size sixteen. Conversely, my clothes are in good shape and generally run at a size fourteen (well, alright, perhaps occasionally somewhat larger).

I admit that she has a few nice pieces that I secretly covet, and there have been times that, without her leave, I have worn. There are even clothes that have price tags still attached, more proof of her profligate ways. And shoes! Don't even get me started on the shoes she has stashed away in my closet! Four pairs of runners—four! Flip flops, sandals, closed toe, no heel, high heels—she has them all. I have one good pair of runners, some flip flops, and, ok, a few pairs of sandals.

Just when does this woman find time to wear this stuff? More importantly, where? When I am at home—wherever that currently is—I certainly don't see her, nor does the content of my closet change except by my actions. Clearly she is where and whenever I am not.

This woman and her clothes must be called to order. I don't recall agreeing to share my closet space with her and frankly I need it. I have some new stuff—urgently needed—that has to be closeted. Perhaps a purge of her clothing and shoes will teach her to keep out of my space . . .

DEADHEADING THE SOUL

At the lake, roses grow along the side of the house leading from the driveway down to the water. While gorgeous when in bloom, they have their waves of growth and decay. What one week was a branch full of buds can be full of flowers past their bloom by the next. No longer having the promise of future budding, these must be removed to make way for new growth. This is the process of deadheading. A careful examination of each plant, each branch, for spent flowers and their removal.

This is my job. A commitment I made when I planted the roses: to keep them healthy, to give them what they need to bloom, and to take away the remains. Deadheading is a time of connection to each plant—an examination of its condition, admiration of its beauty, and an assessment of what it needs to thrive. There is judgement too. Do I remove this flower or not? Is this branch dead wood that needs to be lopped off? When I am done deadheading and pruning, I step back to admire the result. The roses look lighter, and it is easier to see the potential for new growth.

Yesterday as I began my task of deadheading, it occurred to me that what is required for the healthy life of my roses might well be required for a healthy soul. My soul in fact. That part of me that carries the eternal from this life to another.

While deadheading the tangible—my roses—was simple enough, just how was I to go about deadheading the intangible? Where do

I look for my soul to see if it needs some attention? I turned to meditation for guidance.

I practise meditation as time spent in the now with myself as I am. It is a time of quietness and stillness. I connect with all that I am: my body, my emotions, and my spirit. I travel inward on waves of quiet awareness to ask, *How am I today?* Or to ask nothing at all, to just be and appreciate what is there.

I think spiritual deadheading may require more of me. To ask this question: *What do I need to let go of in order to thrive?* Then listen and wait for answers. I suspect that I will find old hurts lurking in corners and resentments I have kept close, finding comfort in bitterness. To release them I must make peace with them. To understand that, whatever purpose they once served, the time has come to let go. To make room for growth.

I can do this, I thought. *I deserve nothing less.*

I stood up, picked up my shears, and went back to tending my roses.

ONCE UPON A TIME

Once upon a time. That's how stories usually start, right? *Once upon a time there was a beautiful princess or a mighty king or a dainty fairy or an ugly old witch.* It's a way to invite the reader into a world created by words. The words can be spoken. They can be sung. They can be written. It doesn't matter. The magic is in the words themselves: *Once upon a time.* This story I am creating for you happens to be a true story about a girl who wanted to be thin. So let us begin.

Once upon a time, there was a young girl, Libby, who lived with her mother, father, and sister above their grocery shop in a small town. The mother and father had stopped loving each other and argued a lot. The sister was a good girl who loved her little sister and took care of her.

One day Libby's mother could not walk anymore and had to go into hospital. Libby was four when that happened. Her sister was in school, and her father worked all day in the grocery store. So, Libby was mostly by herself. She was often bored so she would look in the refrigerator or in the cupboards for something to eat. If she didn't see anything she liked, she would go down through the back hallway to the store and get something there. Libby didn't make good choices about food. She liked cookies, so she ate cookies. A lot of cookies. She liked hamburgers and ice cream, so when her father gave her money to go and buy lunch she would go to the confectionary and buy a hamburger and an ice cream cone. At night, Libby would often feel lonely because she missed her mother. Eating made the loneliness go away, so Libby would make a sandwich and eat it in bed. Libby got fatter and fatter. Soon people were talking about how fat she was—right in front of her, as though being fat meant that she couldn't hear.

When she was six years old, Libby was put on a diet by her doctor. *You are too fat*, he said.

Libby cried when she told her father what the doctor had said.

Her father laughed and said, *Well, he's right.*

Libby didn't have anyone to explain what a diet was or what she should eat instead of cookies and hamburgers and ice cream. So, she kept on eating what she liked. She got fatter.

Eventually Libby's mother came home in a wheelchair. Her mother made good food for the family, and for a while Libby gave up eating cookies. She was frightened, though, by the loud arguments between her mother and father that made her mother cry and try to go down the twenty-two steps from the apartment to the ground, on her bottom. When this happened, Libby and her sister had to sit with their mother and comfort her and then help her back into her wheelchair. Afterwards, Libby would sneak something from the kitchen to eat in her bedroom.

When Libby went to school, teachers discovered that she was smart. So smart that Libby skipped Grade 1 and went right into Grade 3. The other kids in Grade 3 were older than Libby and made fun of her because she was young, too smart, and way too fat. Libby saved herself by being funny and making people laugh, often at her. That's what fat people had to do, she discovered. Be funny so that people would want to be around them even though they were fat. Inside, Libby felt small and empty. Food filled in the spaces, so she didn't hurt as much.

Libby's mother was in and out of hospital a lot. When she was home, she did worry about Libby's weight and tried to get her to eat less and exercise more. She put Libby in tap dancing lessons with other girls who were thinner. They laughed at Libby when her legs shook. Her mother began talking with other mothers about how worried she was about Libby and discussed what to do about her. Right in front of Libby. Libby felt ashamed because, apparently, it was all her fault that she was so fat. It was like a character flaw.

By high school the family had moved into a new house. Libby's mother and father still were not talking to each other, and when they did, it was to argue. They said hurtful things about the other to Libby, leaving her confused and wondering what to do. The good sister had gone to university, so Libby was mostly alone with her unhappy parents. She had learned to eat in secret so that people couldn't criticize or take the food away. Libby loved to read, and the very best thing was to snuggle in bed with a good book and a sandwich or a chocolate bar. So that's what she did. Libby had perfected being funny and so she did have friends to hang out with. Being smart meant praise and good marks at school so that was a safe place to be—except for physical education, which was a nightmare. At home, Libby escaped into books and humoured her mother by trying all sorts of exercises like rolling across the rug to reduce her thighs. This was humiliating, but Libby had discovered that fat people should expect to be humiliated, as being fat was their own fault.

On her seventeenth birthday her family gave her a membership to a spa where Libby could exercise and get help with her diet. At first Libby was embarrassed by the gift, but she decided to go. Libby's world changed. The spa staff were all very thin and beautiful but nice enough and encouraging. They told Libby to eat meat and vegetables and nothing else, to avoid anything with sugar in it. They taught Libby how to use the exercise equipment. Soon Libby started to lose weight and she went to the spa every day. Within three months, Libby had lost so much weight that people started to notice and congratulate her. This made Libby even more determined to watch what she ate and exercise hard. She discovered that it was easier just not to eat rather than watch what and how much. So, she ate very little, and then only meat and maybe plain lettuce. Soon Libby was nearing the weight she was supposed to be, and people told her how good she looked. That made her feel great. She stopped having to be funny to have friends and even had a boyfriend. Libby could find clothes that fit her in the cool stores other girls shopped in. She looked like them. For the first time, Libby's mother and father were proud of her for something more than how smart she was.

Libby kept losing weight. So much weight in fact that now her mother was pestering her to eat. By this time, Libby had come to hate food and viewed those who insisted that she eat as her enemies. If she was made to eat, to be polite or to get her mother off her back, she did, but then went into the bathroom and threw up. This, Libby found, was an effective way to be able to eat a little but stay very thin.

She went to university and enjoyed the freedom of being away from her family and people watching to make sure that she ate. So, she didn't. Not much anyway. She needed to save calories for drinking beer with the other kids. Libby found going to classes tiring—she needed a lot of sleep by now. Still, she was doing well enough to get by. Not eating or eating then throwing up took time and Libby was devoted to keeping thin. She was thrilled that she was much skinnier than most of the girls and that you could see her ribs and her hip bones through her clothes. If people expressed concern, Libby lied and said that she had always been thin, and it was nothing to worry about. One day Libby went into Student Health to get some medicine for a cold. Waiting to sign in, she became dizzy and passed out. When she came to, she was in a hospital bed with an IV in her arm.

Libby was eighteen years old and five feet, six inches tall, and weighed eighty-eight pounds. Her body was literally starving to death, she was told. She had passed out because she was dehydrated and had no calories to burn for energy. The doctor said she had to weigh at least 115 pounds before she could leave the hospital. Libby was terrified at the thought of putting on weight. She wanted to stay thin forever. So, she refused to eat. She refused to eat until the doctor said that he would have to tube feed her. The thought of a tube going down her throat or directly into her stomach was so horrific that Libby agreed to eat. They brought her some tomato soup and she had five tablespoons before she started sobbing.

The psychologist who saw Libby three times a week at the hospital wanted her family to get involved. *They own some of this*, the psychologist said. Libby knew that this was a bad idea, as her mother would be embarrassed and blame Libby's father, or Libby herself, and Libby's father would be bored and want to get back to the store. The psychologist insisted, though, and Libby's parents dutifully came. Just as Libby predicted, her mother was angry and her father was distracted.

After the meeting Libby said to the psychologist, *I will never do that again.* She started losing weight.

As Libby was in the university hospital, there were limited beds and meals prepared by an onsite cook by the name of Maggie. Libby found this out one day when she was wandering around the halls with nothing to do, having had to withdraw from her university classes. When she poked her head into the kitchen, Maggie smiled and said, *Come in and have a coffee. You're Libby, right?*

So, she went into Maggie's kitchen and had a cup of coffee. Maggie did not mention Libby's weight, nor did she try to make her eat something. Instead, she sat down and chatted away, talking about what it was like being a cook, asking Libby what she liked to do and where she was from.

Libby went to visit Maggie every day after that. Sometimes she would help Maggie cook and began tasting the things they were making. Food started to taste good again, and when Maggie would put a plate of sandwiches on the table when they sat down for coffee, Libby would sometimes eat one or two. Maggie made Libby feel warm inside, loved and accepted for herself. She could tell Maggie things that she kept from her psychologist, and Maggie would listen. Maggie would hug Libby and whisper, *You are fine just as you are, honey.*

Finally, Libby weighed 115 pounds and was released from hospital. She was afraid to be on her own and very sad to be leaving Maggie. If she was more confident now, it was because of Maggie. If she felt loved now, it was because of Maggie. What her parents and her psychologist and even her good sister were unable to do, Maggie had done. So, Libby gave Maggie one last hug and went out into the world to live her life.

Have you figured out that Libby is really me and that this is my story? I thought that you might, but it was easier to tell you in the third person. I wish that I could end it with, *and she lived happily ever after.* In a way that is true. I have had a good life. I adore my husband, who tells me every day that I am the most beautiful girl in the world. Together we have raised great kids and now are grandparents to even better granddaughters. I had a successful career.

Weight has been a constant battle, and obesity has usually won the skirmishes. It is a sore point with me so that, if a health professional or an acquaintance raises the issue or if I hear myself described as being "heavy," I retreat into silence where I am attacked by hurt and self-loathing. It is my Achilles heel, and I don't want to discuss it. Except I told you, didn't I? I think I wanted you to understand my story and, if you relate to it, to give you a hug.

LIST(LESS)

Early in our marriage, James and I came to an agreement regarding assignment of "Things to Be Done." As I clearly occupied the position of "Type A Person Most Likely to Fret," my job was to *make* lists. With a few notable exceptions, James' job was to *do* the things on the lists. By and large this was a good system except for the fact that the *maker* of the list was supposed to trust that the *doer* would deliver. I was not good at this part of the process, especially as my husband tended to forget that a list was in play and needed to be completed. This led to lively domestic discussions, particularly when the lists had to do with an upcoming trip:

Me: Did you pick up the dry cleaning?

James: What dry cleaning? You never told me to pick up the dry cleaning.

Me: It was on the "Things to Do Before Going" list.

James: I have never seen a "Things to Do Before Going" list. I have a "Things to Buy Before Packing" list and a "Things to Worry About" list. You *never gave me* a "Things to Do Before Going" list.

Me (somewhat hotly): I most certainly did give you a "Things to Do Before Going" list; it had getting some pesos and dog food on it.

James (accusingly): Pesos? You most certainly *did not* give me any list with pesos on it.

Matters usually deteriorated from there.

To our credit we generally managed to clear the lists and get everything in order before leaving on vacation.

Over the years we travelled a fair bit with our kids and then, when they left, on our own. Every trip was preceded by prodigious list-making but now it's done on a more equitable basis. James and I make the lists *together* and assign responsibilities *together*. I still can't resist checking on his progress, though I am making headway, and leave it to the very last moment to say, "Did you pick up the dry cleaning?"

Someday, maybe, we will get to the point of not needing to make a pre-holiday list. We will become those type of freewheeling folks who throw a few things in a bag before heading to the airport, knowing that if they forgot something, they can always buy what they need at the other end. I dream of being that list-less person who is prepared to take a risk and go without if need be. Maybe someday I will get there, but for now, it is enough that the lists are getting shorter.

THE STOCKINGS WERE HUNG ON
THE PORTHOLE WITH CARE

In the beginning was the Word.

"Swannie and I," said my mother-in-law, "are thinking about taking all of you on a cruise to celebrate our 50th anniversary."

"All of you" meant her children, their spouses, and their children—eighteen of us in total. The cruise turned out to be a seven-day tour of the Western Caribbean. The only snag was that it included Christmas Eve and Christmas Day, and my seven-year-old son was not impressed.

Sometime in November, curled up in front of the TV watching the cruise video for the tenth time, Zander poked my arm and said, "I am not going." Now, in many ways, Zander is our most easygoing child, content to fall in with family plans. However, his slender body housed a will of iron (my side), resolute stubbornness (my husband's side), and the ability to be absolutely unreasonable (his own contribution to the genetic soup). Once engaged, these traits spelled TROUBLE.

Attempting to head it off, I hunkered down beside him and in my most soothing tones said, "Honey, why on earth would you say that?"

"Because," he answered, his brow furrowing mightily, "I'm just not going to."

Apparently, he had also inherited his father's way with words.

Several days later, the boycott was still on. Determined to get to the root of his opposition, I sat him down across from me.

"Can you please tell Mommy why you don't want to go on the cruise?"

"Because I just don't want to, that's why."

"Alexander, that is not very helpful. If you don't tell Mommy right this minute why you do not want to go on this cruise *that I have been slaving away to get ready for*, we will just leave you behind with a babysitter!"

"Ok. I don't want to go on the cruise because Santa will not know where we are, and I won't get any presents. That, and we will probably drown because the ship will sink. What's a babysitter anyway?"

Although I never did convince him that the ship was unlikely to sink, we did make headway on the issue of Santa Claus by sending off a letter advising him that on Christmas Eve we would be at sea. Would he please consider dropping off the presents at the ship?

The much-anticipated day of boarding the ship finally came. It was Christmas Eve, and after a busy few hours of exploring the ship, it was time to return to our cabin to await the call to muster. This entailed finding our life jackets, reading the instructions on the back of our closet door, and trying to convince a disgruntled Zander that mustering would be lots and lots of fun. That, even though we had to wear life jackets and stand by the lifeboats, there was nothing to worry about. Try telling this to a boy who had based an entire boycott on the premise that ships sink. I could tell that he wasn't buying any of it from the scowl etched across his forehead and the definite droop to his lower lip.

Seven short blasts followed by one long one—our call to muster. Down the hall and up the stairs to Deck Seven. Out the doors to Muster Station #1. A patient crew member stood ready to assemble a ragtag bunch of bewildered passengers into something vaguely resembling an evacuation team. "Form a line please, according to your cabins, if you can," he instructed. "Children first, then women, men at the back."

Zander most definitely did *not* please to do anything. It took my blackest look coupled with a firm arm hold to convince him to put on his life jacket. Thrust into the front of our line, as instructed, he dove through my legs and back to his father who, in fine seaman tradition, had found a deck chair in which to muster. I did my best to look like I belonged to a more obedient line.

Mustering over, the ship left port and headed out to sea. Back at our cabin, we began the process of unpacking our luggage. I opened the suitcase containing—quite literally—our Christmas. Out came the familiar Christmas stockings, one for each of us. These I handed to Zander, who solemnly hung stocking loops over the nut lugs of the porthole. Underneath the stockings we set up a small crèche, no bigger than the palm of my hand. Beside that went a photo album full of Christmases past.

Zander breathed a sigh of relief and his little body relaxed for the first time that day. "Do you really think Santa will find us, Mommy?" he asked, looking up at me with concerned eyes.

"Oh yes I do, son," I answered confidently. "In fact I am sure of it."

We settled down to read *How the Grinch Stole Christmas*. Before I could begin, however, Zander grinned up at me. "Hey Mom—the stockings were hung by the *porthole* with care. Get it?"

I got it all right and gave him a quick hug, celebrating the enduring magic of Christmas. I had much the same thought later that night as I joined hundreds of my fellow passengers for a carol sing in the Centrum area. Led by entertainment staff and accompanied by a live orchestra, our voices wound down the circular stairwell, sometimes lively and more often quiet and reflective. At sea and with strangers for the most part, I felt among friends as Christmas Eve became Christmas Day.

I am pleased to say that Santa did indeed find the ship and Zander awoke to filled stockings and lots of presents. Better still, Santa even managed a visit to the ship later that afternoon, bringing even more presents for the kids aboard.

That night as I tucked him in, Zander whispered, "Santa is so special, right mom? No matter where you are, if you let him know, he will find you."

"Christmas has a way of finding all of us, honey," I whispered back. "It always does."

TALES FROM OCHO RIOS: THE CHRISTMAS CRUISE PART 2

Our extended-family Western Caribbean Cruise took us to four ports of call, including Ocho Rios, Jamaica. This was a deepwater port so we were able to disembark directly onto the pier and, having decided to give excursions a miss, thought to spend the day just wandering around the city.

The day dawned clear and bright. *A good omen*, I thought, followed by, *what a way to start the morning off!* as I was handed a rum punch by a pretty young Jamaican woman running the Board of Tourism stand.

Four of us, James, me, and the two boys, would spend the day together while Jenn had plans with the other teenagers. We took a taxi from the dock to the shopping area and wandered around for a bit, purchasing T-shirts and trinkets along the way.

In an open air crafts market, our ten-year-old, Ben, was immediately drawn to a wood carver's stall, strung with hand carved wooden masks. Knowing that buying such a mask was high on his list, I guessed that he was going to be occupied for a while. Even at a young age, Ben had the ability to dig in and stay the course to get what he wanted—and at the best possible price. There was no one else in the stall. Just Ben and the wood carver, grizzled and dark, sitting on a stump, working on a new mask. Ben moved closer to the carver and hunkered down by this side. The man smiled at him, pleased, I think, at Ben's interest in what he was doing and Ben's ease at being so close.

James and I stood silently by, giving them space but keeping an eye on our son.

After a few minutes of watching quietly, Ben began a conversation. "So you like to whittle, do ya? I like to whittle, too. Wanna see my new Swiss Army knife?"

I thought I saw the guy wince at the word "whittle," but I couldn't be sure and turned away quickly before someone identified me as whittler's mother.

Our Ben was a talker. Once started, he was unlikely to move on until he accomplished his mission which, in this case, was to buy a mask. Before long a deal had been struck. Ben bought a carved mask at a good price and in return agreed to go and befriend someone else. When we asked the carver to sign the back of the mask, he went further and took up his chisel to stencil the date and the inscription: *Ben-the-Guard*. We have pictures of Ben holding his mask, standing beside its creator: a sturdy blond child and a grizzled Jamaican bound by artistry and mercantilism.

We moved on, taking in the sights, sounds, and smells of a Jamaican market. Rum punch was readily available to ensure that James and I maintained a mellow mood and the boys loved the fresh fruit juice.

Just up ahead was a bit of a ruckus. A woman yelling in full, rich tones, "Girl, you get back here! You want to take my picture—you gotta pay me first!" The woman was a more rounded version of Carmen Miranda, complete with ruffled skirt, billowed sleeves, and a cloth head wrapping with what looked to be fruit and flowers. She was shaking her fists and waddling quickly after the girl in question, who was running straight toward us.

"Help me, Mom," Jenn hollered as she fled from her pursuer.

Safely hidden behind her father, Jenn clutched his middle.

I stepped forward to intercept Ms. Miranda. "Is there a problem?" I asked.

"This your girl?" she demanded.

"It is. What did she do?" I enquired.

"She took my picture without paying me first. That's my job—I get dressed up and then people pay to take my picture. This girl didn't even ask. She just took the picture and then when I told her to pay, she ran off." The woman was incensed.

"Hmm. I see your point. She was probably just frightened. How much do you usually charge?"

We reached an agreement as to price—not much—and I added a healthy tip to make amends. We parted on good terms, though Jenn remained shaken for a while.

Rounding a corner, James and I burst into laughter. The sight of our daughter running for her life while being chased by a stout Jamaican woman dressed to the nines, shaking her head so that the fruit on her headdress wobbled alarmingly, was hilarious.

We returned to the ship, full of good food and clutching our respective treasures from the markets. Our day in Ocho Rios left us rich in memories, and we never fail to laugh when we recall our encounter with Carmen Miranda.

OUR MEXICAN HOME

It is cocktail time—*la hora de los amigos*—in our little Mexican town of Mahahual. The sun is setting over the ocean, casting purple shadows on the turquoise waters of the Caribbean. I dig my bare feet into the still-warm sand beneath the plastic table and take another drink of my margarita. My husband and I watch the waves break on the coral reef before moving lazily towards shore. Overhead, pelicans spread their wings and ride the updrafts created by cooling air passing over warm water. *We live here*, we say to each other, still surprised by the truth of that statement. *This is home.*

And so it is. For all the winter months we can manage, we are at our house in Mahahual, a cruise port town and former fishing village about five hours southeast of Cancún, in the frontier state of Quintana Roo, Mexico. Houses have names here as well as numbers. We named our house *El Garaje Azul* because it is a house that grew out of a desire to build a workshop and a garage as an adjunct to our oceanfront condominium. My garden is full of tropical plants and flowers that you can only buy at florists back home in Canada. James has just finished building a small pool in our backyard—a promise he made when we left the condo with its amazing pool overlooking the sea.

Mahahual has changed me. I am growing more patient. I can almost accept that I am not completely in control here, and that is difficult for a former corporate lawyer to do. I am softer and more vulnerable because the people here treat me with such kindness and openheartedness that I can offer them nothing less in return. When my inadequate Spanish fails me, I offer hugs instead of words. Mahahual has taught me to need less, to take chances, and to lean on my friends when I must.

We didn't go looking for Mahahual or for any other place in Mexico. It instead found us, falling into our lives as a result of friendship and, well, fate, I suppose. We came to know of Mahahual through good friends who had a long-standing relationship with the area and eventually, after Hurricane Dean, built a house here. That fact coupled with our growing appreciation of this small town led to buying property here—first a lot, then a condominium right on the ocean, and finally, *El Garaje Azul*, the house we built on our lot when condominium life became too restrictive.

If our discovery of Mahahual was by chance, our love for the town grew out of experiences and relationships. Like any love affair, it began with an attraction to the obvious: the Caribbean with its turquoise waters, the warmth of the Yucatán sun, and the somewhat cheaper cost of living.

To develop an enduring relationship and a connection with any place, you must, I think, do more than just spend time there. You must also invest a little bit of your soul. The sheer physical beauty of Mahahual prompts many to make their home here. They need nothing more than the beach, the ocean, and the sun. That attracts us too, but it is the people and our interactions with them and their lives that touch us the most. They have become our storekeepers, our neighbours, and our friends. We make memories with them.

Our circle of friends is a mixed bag of *Mexicanos* and ex-pats, some who live in Mahahual full time, some who are seasonal residents like we are. The Indigenous population where we live is primarily Mayan and there are still places where the Mayan language, rather than Spanish, is dominant. We have learned so much about the history and culture of Costa Maya—and of Mexico for that matter—through conversations with friends and sometimes store owners, waiters, and even taxi drivers when they have the time and inclination to talk. We are grateful for such instruction. In our view, we have been welcomed into their country and benefit from our experiences here. It is a small price to pay to try to learn the language, history, and culture of the place we both call home.

The ex-pat community around Mahahual is made up of primarily Americans, Europeans, Canadians, and South Americans. I have noticed similarities amongst us regardless of our country of origin: adaptability, openness to adventure, and a charming tendency towards eccentricity.

Some of the most interesting, creative, and intelligent women I have ever met live in and around Mahahual. We get together for lunch, yoga, and art classes, or to sip cocktails as the sun goes down. I love these ladies, and in retirement I have time to spend with them.

James and I look to these folks for advice and help in navigating everyday life. Where to get the car fixed, where to find wheat flour, who to call to fix the plumbing, how much to pay and on what terms, and the exact meaning of *mañana*. Life in Mahahual—essentially a rural town when there are no ships in port—can be a challenge. Not only does the language issue complicate things, but you also often cannot find what you need.

When we bought the condo and later built the house, there were things that we needed or wanted that we couldn't find at an acceptable price or quality in Quintana Roo. We did what all ex-pats do and began hauling things from home. Stainless steel screws and fixtures for sinks and showers were easy enough. The sinks themselves and over-the-stove microwaves were a different story. So were MixMasters, battery chargers, and tools. We have transported them all. The sight of supposed tourists lugging three or four hockey bags through the airport baggage area has resulted in many interesting conversations with Mexican customs agents.

Fluency in Spanish has also been an issue. While Canada has two official languages, neither is Spanish. James and I came to Mexico with a few key phrases like *hola* and *cuánto cuesta*. Over the years, our vocabulary has certainly improved, but we are nowhere near fluency despite our daily online language lessons. Instead, we rely on Spanish-speaking friends to act as our interpreters when understanding and being understood really matters. James has also become proficient at charades, accompanied—for some reason—by short whistles, which other guys seem to be able to interpret. This system works especially well at the local hardware store, where he has developed quite a following.

My fluency is somewhat more advanced, and I can sometimes manage short conversations. That said, I have had my own run-ins with the language—much to my embarrassment—like the time I was trying to find white carpenter's glue. An earlier experience trying to find Krazy Glue (sold as *Kola Loco)* led me to believe that the word for glue must be *kola*. Content with this logic, I concluded that white glue would be *kola blanca*. I asked for *kola blanca* at our local stationary store and at several larger stores in Chetumal only to be given frosty, often hostile glares. When I tried our local hardware store, the guy at the counter (who spoke English), and most of the customers hanging around, burst out laughing. Turns out the correct word for glue is *pegamento*. *Kola* was local slang for "bum" or, more crudely, "ass." I had been asking seemingly decent people all over our town and in Chetumal if they had "white ass." I could have died.

Lord only knows what James and I have been saying in our well-meaning but hopelessly flawed attempts to respect the country we are living in by speaking its language. Mostly people seem to appreciate that we are trying, and even if they can't understand us, we are able to laugh together. Our inability and reluctance to speak Spanish, though, has made everyday tasks more complicated—like arranging to have our propane tank filled. We use propane for our stove and water heater. A tankful lasts maybe a month, sometimes less. Although it is possible to simply call and arrange for delivery, our inability to speak and understand Spanish, particularly over the phone, inhibits us from doing so. Instead, my husband engages in a process that goes like this: First is an acknowledgment that we are almost out of propane, which leads to the placing of a large "GAS" sign on the road outside of our house or, if we are desperate, at the corner where our street meets the main road. We alert our pals, who let us know if the gas truck has been sighted in town. James himself then goes out. Eventually, there will be a "sighting," and the chase is on. If the truck is close enough, James will run after it, his arms waving wildly. Usually this is enough for the truck to stop, and a delivery is arranged. Sometimes, however, more effort is required. James rushes home for our car and pursues the gas truck that way. Neighbours have been known to become involved. There is a deep sense of accomplishment and satisfaction when the truck pulls up outside of our house and fills the tank. The rest of the day can be treated as a holiday, with no more work needed to call it a success.

These experiences and so many more have not only made us resilient, they are the stuff of memories that, with time, make us laugh or remind us of times when we had to dig deep or rely on others to make our life in Mahahual possible.

This will be our sixth year living part time in Mahahual. When I retired and it became possible to make Mahahual our winter home, it also became clear that condo living was not going to work for my husband. James is a project guy. He likes to build and repair things, and for that he needed a workshop and things that needed to be built or repaired. We also had a truck that needed to be protected from humidity and salt air. We decided to build on our lot. We found an amazing general contractor who had relocated from Mexico City, signed a contract, and within a year we were able to move in. For the most part, everything went smoothly, and the house was built on budget and on time. Still, the plumbing and the electrical wiring are a bit wonky—there are few standards and no inspections to speak of—and the roof leaks. James is kept busy and never complains about having nothing to do.

A Canadian and a Mexican flag fly over our house. We are proud to be Canadians and we are grateful to also have a life in Mahahual. When we open the street door and enter our magical courtyard, we are home. Friends drop by, or we go to see them. We shop for groceries at our favourite *tienda*, see the local doctor when we need to, and have cocktails on the beach. There is time for swimming in the ocean, time for meaningful conversations and confusing ones when we try to speak Spanish.

James still chases the gas man.

THE STRANGER AT MY DOOR

I am a huge fan of online shopping and have been for quite a while. Throughout my law career I was often too busy for in-person shopping or, quite frankly, found that a quick trip to, say, the Amazon site offered respite from an otherwise boring day. Now in retirement and living in rural areas in both Mexico and Canada, online shopping is a necessity. While online shopping might be a blow to the local economy, that is a consequence I am prepared to live with. There is another upside to online shopping: the arrival of lovely packages to your door, the contents of which have long escaped your memory.

Although rapid—even one-day—turnaround is increasingly common, the usual time delay between placing my order and delivery is sufficient for me to have forgotten all about it. When the package arrives, it is as a delightful surprise: a present for me, as it were, from me. Nothing gladdens my heart more than to arrive home to find a parcel or two propped up by the door. Picking up the mail is less of a chore when there is a possibility of a delivery notice. And let me not overlook the excitement of a knock on the door.

This is particularly the case at our house in Mexico. Deliveries there are usually preceded by a text or email foreshadowing arrival that very day. Mexico being what it is, that message is quite often followed by a later one, indicating that delivery will occur "tomorrow." Nonetheless, I have a great deal of fondness for these strangers who bring me the goods I apparently ordered and now have forgotten about. So dedicated are they that we were once tracked down by our (usual) driver in Mexico at a local bar, all so he could make his delivery. While we try to be generous with our tips, I feel somehow that this isn't enough. That I should perhaps enquire after his family, ask him in for a beverage or a quick snack, get to know him a little. As it is, my husband (who typically answers the door) and the delivery man are on quite friendly terms and often have an extended chat curbside.

So, here's to those intrepid men and women who make online shopping possible. Whose deliveries gladden my heart and brighten my day. I am devoted to their continued prosperity and job security. I have no plans to quit this habit anytime soon.

MISILE

I never knew his real name. Our friends simply called him Misile for reasons unknown to me. I think he was a Mexican nationalist, but again, that is just a guess. He was an alcoholic and homeless, typically camping in the bush in *Las Casitas* in our winter hometown of Mahahual. Everyone knew or recognized him, and he, in turn, greeted everyone with an infectious smile and a wave of his hand.

Just the fact of Misile made Mahahual more real and homier to me. We weren't here on vacation. This was a place where we were trying to put down roots. Mahahual was made up of real people leading real lives. Misile was one of those people. Knowing who he was, having him wave at us, and waving back in return meant that we belonged; we were *locals*.

Homeless he might be, but for a while Misile had a car washing business. He even had flyers printed off. Lacking a base, the location of the service varied from day to day, but it was always in Las Casitas. His equipment consisted of a pail filled with water (and sometimes soap) and rags. With that and elbow grease, Misile returned your car sparkling clean.

He sometimes showed up as a waiter in one of the local restaurants. Word was that at one time, before the booze, he had been a server in some of the classiest restaurants in Cancún. You could hire Misile to do casual labour like yard work by the hour but only in the mornings. Afternoons and evenings were devoted to drinking.

His fall had been spectacular, but he seemed to embrace the life he now had.

There was a story told about Misile and Hurricane Dean. Apparently, he was locked up in the local jail for some misdemeanour when it became clear that the hurricane was going to hit Mahahual hard. As everyone in town was evacuating inland, the local authorities offered to release Misile and forgive the rest of his sentence, provided that he stayed in town throughout the storm and kept an eye on things.

This he did, even though flood waters were waste deep even a kilometre back from the shore.

We came back to Mahahual one year to find out that Misile had been banished from town for some suspected wrongdoing and had returned to Cancún where he reportedly died. I found his loss incredibly sad, as though Mahahual had lost something vital and bright. This is my farewell to this little man with the huge smile and an approach to life that, even through addiction, shone.

THE COFFEE AFFAIR

We spend the winter months at our home in Mexico. One of our good friends there is a dynamo entrepreneur. Kay is willing to tackle anything that has money-making potential. She has had restaurants, cafés, bakeries, and a catering business; sold pizza; and is currently in the live plant business. One of her enduring ventures is selecting, packaging, and selling her own brand of coffee. Her coffee is well known in and around Mahahual, the town where we both live, but Kay was interested in expanding her market, notably to the United States and Canada.

Our oldest granddaughter, back home in Canada, was trying to raise money for a school trip. I decided that selling Kay's coffee as a fundraiser would be just the thing to help both out. We were going home soon and would be able to haul the coffee with us. Simple enough, we thought, as the hockey bags we stuffed with all sorts of stuff to bring down to Mexico were now empty. We loaded one with more than forty one-kilogram bags of coffee and headed confidently to our flight from Cancún to Edmonton.

Arrival was straightforward as always. We easily got through immigration and headed to the luggage carousel. No hockey bag. I wandered around, thinking perhaps it had been relocated to the oversize baggage area and, sure enough, there it was. The moment I put my hand on it, two very large, very official-looking RCMP officers appeared and asked if this was my bag. Confirming that it was, I asked if there was an issue. There apparently was, and it had to do with the large amount of coffee the bag contained. Apparently, and certainly unbeknownst to us, coffee is used to disguise the smell of drugs. The officers' suspicions were heightened by the added presence of duct tape in the bag, another indicator that we were drug smugglers.

By this time James had joined me and we both looked askance at the offending bag. I launched into a very detailed and animated account of our friend, her attempts to make a living in Mexico, how great the coffee was (sustainably grown, hand-picked, and so on), our granddaughter needing to raise money for a school trip, and my great idea of selling Kay's coffee. James then took on explaining the presence of duct tape. He always travelled with duct tape, he offered, in case of luggage or other travel-related issues. He just happened to toss it into the hockey bag at the last minute. The officers listened attentively and seemed to accept our explanations. We clearly were either the stupidest drug smugglers in history or telling the truth.

Nonetheless, random bags of coffee had to be opened and tested. For the briefest of moments, I panicked. How well did I really know Kay? What if we had unwittingly become middle-aged mules for drugs? I began to sweat heavily.

Testing the bags seemed to take forever. James and I stood by silently, trying to not look like criminals. The results confirmed the presence of coffee and nothing else. *Phew*, I thought.

The officers, now openly laughing, let us go, dragging the coffee-filled hockey bag behind us like chastened children.

After all that, our granddaughter's trip was cancelled and no fundraising was needed. We have yet to run out of coffee.

POTHOLES AND OTHER MEXICAN HORROR STORIES

With the help of a flashlight, James and I stared down at the pothole that had just punctured a tire on our rental car. As potholes went, this one wasn't particularly deep or broad. Its nastiness lay in its sharp and jagged edges.

With a deep sigh, James got out the jack and the spare tire. My job was to hold the light so he could see. We were on a beach road, surrounded by jungle. It was dark, and I was distracted by sounds coming from the dense brush. There were *tigres* and wild boar and other strange and dangerous animals in those bushes, I knew. My light-holding duties were divided between illuminating the road and flash examinations of the jungle.

Beach roads and secondary rural roads in and around our Mexican town are notorious for potholes. In fact, the roads are more often a series of interconnected potholes than a driving surface. Maneuvering a vehicle requires the ability to see a path around them or, if that is not possible, to choose those less likely to cause damage. Locals seem less intimidated than those of us from town. While we carefully edge our way over the top of the next pothole, one wheel at a time, a local vehicle might pass us, bouncing and crashing through the course. Cars don't typically last a long time in our part of Mexico. What doesn't rust in the salty, humid air eventually falls apart from pothole abuse. You really can't blame the roads. They are superimposed on boggy wetlands never intended to support vehicle traffic. Construction is often haphazard and done on a budget by developers or residents wanting to access beachfront property. Maintenance is spotty at best and left to the locals to take care of.

It is not unusual for entire conversations to be about potholes: where the really nasty ones are, what might be done about them, and whose car has been wiped out recently.

Some reach celebrity status. The pothole at Kilometre 47, for example, was so deep that a random road sign stuck down it barely cleared the surface. Its infamy spread by word of mouth. We all knew about it, although it could sneak up on you if you were driving after sunset through its habitat—an unlit patch of jungle road.

Some ingenious measures have been taken to fill in potholes, short of a true repair. We have seen old tires shoved down inside a pothole if it is one of the broad but not too deep ones. Lumber has been used as well, though with limited success. I have often thought that packing potholes with the ubiquitous garbage might kill two birds with one stone but, so far, my idea has not met with much enthusiasm.

When the local community rallies and undertakes a repair of a road, there is much joy and cause for celebration. We all rush to drive down it, just for the thrill of not having to deal with potholes. Congratulations are extended to the community members, who, quite rightly, feel flush with having seen to their responsibility. No one seems to question why this a job for residents and not for the municipal government, which, after all, collects our taxes.

Like many things about our life in Mexico, potholes just have to be accepted for what they are. You adjust your expectations for how long it will take to drive to the beach, you avoid driving after sunset, and whenever possible, you travel in groups. The drive, however

hazardous, is worth it once you get to the beach and see the ocean—
it never fails to take my breath away—and suddenly potholes seem
a small price to pay.

HOW I (ALMOST) READ THOREAU'S WALDEN

Last year I decided to take a break from chick lit and read something brainy. Thoreau's *Walden; or, Life in the Woods* came to mind, having been quoted in a book I had just finished. I vaguely recalled that the brainier (and weirder) guys at university reverentially referred to it as a "transcendental classic." I decided to give it a go.

A few pages in and I remembered why I avoid reading improving books, especially those written in the nineteenth century. Though likely full of big ideas and useable quotes, reading Thoreau was akin to slogging through a muddy bog. Nonetheless, determined to be enlightened instead of entertained by my reading, I plowed on.

By the end of the first chapter, I had caught the cadence of his writing style and reading became a little easier. Instead of being stupefied, I was becoming indignant. *How noble of him*, I thought to myself, *to take on a peasant's life to ensure that he wasn't "missing" something essential. Perhaps he should have avoided the experience and simply spoken with people living hand to mouth.* I wondered if I was alone in my condemnation and turned to the Internet. Turns out that *Walden* has its admirers and its detractors, leading to vigorous online debate.

In no time at all I had formed my allegiance (detractors) and turned my energies from reading the book to reading articles on the Internet. Much more interesting and entertaining, I thought, and given frequent references to the work in question, still qualified as "improving reading." My favourite discovery was that his mother "helped him out" with laundry and cooking. Of course she did. What educated gentleman of that period could be expected to cope with such mundane tasks whilst undertaking the noble experiment of living a simple life?

Perhaps a better person would have read on, if only to be able to claim that they had read *Walden*. I am cut from weaker cloth, and so, abandoned the book and put it on the bottom of my pile of things to read. My reading time is too important to be spent trying to unravel the meaning of a paragraph and then, once revealed, to be maddened by it. Still, I now feel able to quote from the work and talk randomly about transcendentalism and the like. After all, I *almost* read Walden.

LOSInG IT

Just between you and me, I think that I am losing it. The "it" I am speaking of is, you know, that mental ability thing—*mental acuity*—that's it. My brain seems to be on a work-to-rule protocol, leaving me adrift in conversations, groping for a word I know I know but which is currently unavailable. To me, that is. Others, notably my adult children and teenaged granddaughters, do not seem to have this issue. I notice them rolling their eyes at my verbal clumsiness, and they are quick to point out when my mouth, bereft of its partner, my brain, says something completely stupid. *Just you wait,* I think to myself. Come to think of it, I did the same thing to my parents and grandparents—eye rolling, laughing at and pitying them in their old age.

Now that it is my turn to be losing it, I have developed some strategies to employ when with others.

1. ***Minimize Speech****.* This works well when you aren't in a one-on-one situation where conversation is a two-way thing. You can feign sleep (although this too may be taken as a sign of dotage, so use it only as a last resort) or deep interest in what the other person is saying. This keeps them talking and thus lessens the chance of you saying something inappropriate. If you must speak, keep your sentences short. Better to be terse than illogical.

2. *Change the Subject.* On occasion I completely lose track of what an ongoing conversation is about. My mind, such as it is, has gone off on its own, leaving me behind, defenseless. A good strategy in such circumstances is to change the subject. Rummage around in your memory bank for some topic that might be relevant to the people you are with. You might introduce it with a phrase like "apropos of nothing" or "before I forget."

3. *Distract Them.* This is the "look—a squirrel" technique. Some finesse is required to use it successfully. You need to have something of sufficient interest or urgency to divert the attention of those with whom you are meant to be conversing. If necessary, create the diversion. For example: spill your drink, knock something over, sneeze loudly. At least this will buy you some time to come up with the word you were looking for or remember what the conversation was about.

4. *Be Charming.* Acknowledge your lapse of memory and laugh lightly; perhaps even wave your hands slightly. Say things like "I know, I'm so foolish, aren't I?" or "Heavens, what was I thinking!" Remember the light laughter—this establishes that you are a good sport about the aging thing.

5. *Blame Medication.* One of my favourites. Everyone assumes that older people are on lots of meds, so it is an available tactic even if you only take over-the-counter stuff.

Feel free to use any or all of these and good luck. I have to do something now—can't quite remember what, but I am sure it will occur to me sooner or later. It's the darn meds that my doctor put me on.

THE METAPHYSICAL SMOKER

I grew up during the late 60s and 70s when everybody smoked. Well, almost everybody *I knew* smoked except for some mothers and grandmothers and maybe the minister of our church. Smoking was what you did if you were an adult or a cool teenager. Ashtrays spilling over with ash and used cigarette ends, some stained with lipstick, were standard décor. In more affluent homes, cigarettes were set out in china boxes with a matching lighter standing alongside. People smoked inside of homes and stores, and in cars, buses, and airplanes. People smoked on television shows and in movies.

I can't recall my first cigarette. It must have been when I was fourteen or fifteen because by sixteen—the age when you could legally smoke and legally buy cigarettes—I had been at it for some time. I smoked with my friends. I smoked during class breaks at school. I smoked along with everyone else in houses, in stores, and in cars. One of my favourite Christmas gifts the year I turned seventeen was an onyx lighter, its use elevating me to the status of an established and perhaps even classy smoker. I remember being taught to re-inhale released smoke back through my nose (French smoking) and how to blow smoke rings. I left high school a confirmed and dedicated smoker. I was hooked. Cigarettes were cool and all sorts of institutions, events, and associations proudly claimed manufacturers as sponsors. Advertising for cigarette brands was displayed on television and radio, on the doors and windows of shops, and on the sides of buses.

I smoked my way through college and later law school. I smoked during my first pregnancy. By then, though, smoking was under attack. Generations woke up to the horrors of lung cancer and the shame of exposing others to second-hand smoke. Cigarette manufacturers were no longer sought after for high-profile sponsorships and no-smoking zones were becoming fashionable. Now *quitting* was in. Addicted as I was, I envied those who managed to give up smoking. I tried many times to quit myself with no success. Without smoking in my life, I became anxious and unanchored.

I was around forty when I managed to move my use of nicotine from cigarettes to gum. I chewed ferociously and copiously, enormously proud that I could now identify myself as a "non-smoker." I developed an aversion to the smell of cigarette smoke and would turn away from those with the smell of smoke on their clothing or on their breath. I told myself that using nicotine gum didn't count. I excused my ongoing nicotine dependency on the basis of being high strung and stressed out. My husband and kids supported my habit, terrified of who I might become if I quit.

But give it up I did at the age of sixty-five. I turned to ordinary chewing gum, hard candies, and cough drops. My mouth apparently must be kept occupied at all times to avoid temptation. Do I miss smoking? Oh yes, yes, I do. Apart from the physical addiction, I miss the elegance of the act itself. The selection of the cigarette and the handling of it. Bending to a match or a lighter and the sharpness of the first deep inhalation. I miss the camaraderie amongst smokers and the companionship of a cigarette in the middle of the night when you can't sleep. I remember the beauty of Audrey Hepburn or Bette Davis waving long cigarette holders as they spoke. Don't get me wrong—I am relieved to have given it up. It's just, well, that a part of me—a metaphysical me—is still out there having the best smoke ever.

CIVIL SOCIETY

Bear with me as I rant just a little. I miss civility or at least I miss the practice of etiquette as it was in the 60s and 70s when I was growing up. There were rules then. People were expected to be *appropriate,* meaning that they said and did what people expected them to say and do. There was a shared understanding about what was *acceptable* and what was not. You might not always like the rules, but at least you knew what they were. Staying on the right side of the line guaranteed a place in society. Currently there appears to be more emphasis on individuality and sensibilities. A fascination with *I* and *me.* Taken to an extreme, that leads to a state of incivility—a willingness to sacrifice the good and the comfort of others to the narcissism of the self.

Somewhere along the line, perhaps in the 80s or 90s, the concept of *the majority* became much maligned. Instead of being upheld as a principle of democracy, it was viewed as a weapon of oppression of the few by the many. I get it. As populations became more diverse, there was and still is a need to address issues like racism. As values shifted, we had to make room for and be tolerant of other points of view and other priorities. As a young adult I did my fair share of rule breaking and protesting. I wanted a brave new world. I just didn't want it to be *this* brave new world.

In losing a feel for the collective, we focus on differences rather than similarities. The Internet and other forms of careless mass media have fostered tribalism and encouraged rudeness cloaked by anonymity. Internet behaviour has now spread to offline, in-person communications. Apparently, you can say what you like, regardless of truth or civility, under the banner of *opinion*. You have a right, you say, to your opinion, and I agree. I also think that you must act responsibly and be accountable for that opinion. If that is too much to ask, then keep it to yourself or share it with others who want to hear it.

While I am at it, may I also say that I have little patience with those who seek to impose their own vulnerabilities or priorities on the rest of us. I am not interested in, nor do I condemn, various forms of gender identification or sexuality, for example, but I do object to restraints placed on my own behaviour because of them. I want the freedom to say that someone is expecting a *girl* and to knit a *pink* blanket, not a multi-coloured one. In doing so I mean no offence to someone who wants gender to be an evolving thing. I just don't want that person to interfere with or object to how I see things, or to insist that society accommodate their preferred approach.

I don't know where we are headed. Maybe democracy, in the Platonian sense, is passé. Maybe civility was a convenient disguise for hypocrisy and needed to be replaced. All I know is that I preferred living in times in which you thought before you spoke and considered how your behaviour might impact another before you acted. When people understood that not everyone shared their priorities and points of view and were okay with that. That's all. Too much to ask, do you think?

THE CAR WASH

With my poor peripheral vision and my inability to accurately assess distance, going through an automated car wash is a challenge. To begin with, one has to successfully guide the car into the track. I tend to overthink this bit and, in my anxiety, oversteer so that one set of wheels inevitably misses the mark and has to be wrenched down to where it is supposed to be. Then there is the moment of fear when the car wash instructs you to *let go;* take your hands off the wheel, your foot off the brake, and put the car into neutral. From this point on, you are told to sit back and just enjoy the experience. And usually I do, no longer responsible for anything requiring either coordination or thought. One time, however, such complacency was horribly misplaced.

On this particular day, I had splurged a little and selected the super deluxe option. This went beyond the straightforward wet-soap-rinse and blow dry to include rainbow-coloured suds, cascading water-falls, and a wax. I had just settled down to enjoy the technicoloured show, when things went wrong. Now, well beyond the first soak and perhaps a third of the way down the track, the whole thing ground to a halt. The track stopped progressing my car, the *swish swish* of the enormous fluffy brushes stopped, and there were no fantasy suds sliding down my windows. I was, it appeared, stuck in the middle of a car wash. I waited, dumbstruck. Nothing happened. No one came rushing to my aid, nor did the car wash resume. I felt guilty, like this glitch was somehow my fault. Had I inadvertently stepped on the brake? Touched the steering wheel? Did the car wash somehow *know* that I was, contrary to instructions, interfering? Feeling sure that my interference lay at the heart of the problem, it never occurred to me take control—to simply put the car into drive and get out of there. As far as I was concerned, the car wash was the boss of me and my car. I was heading towards a full-blown panic attack when I saw it—a bright, shiny red button on the adjacent wall labelled "Call for Help." Relieved, I flung open the driver's door and began picking my way over car wash paraphernalia, ducking under suspended hoses and brushes. Then this happened.

The track, still clutching my car, began to move. Jets of water squirted merrily inside through the open door and then multi-coloured foam began its *rat-a-tat-tat* process. Having not made it to the button, I abruptly changed course back to my now-travelling car. That put me squarely in line of the action. I was watered, soaped, and very nearly buffed. Panicked at the thought of my driverless car, I lurched ahead and grabbed hold of the open door as the car happily glided towards its final rinse and wax. I slid in, riding a wave of water swamping the driver's seat, and slammed the door shut. I closed my eyes and put my head on the steering wheel as purple foam dripped down my forehead.

Together again, my car and I exited the car wash. "Have a Nice Day" blinked at me as I shifted into drive and took back control. That apparently was the last straw for my water-addled self as I became seized with the need to "Report This Incident" to the authorities—in this case, a rather horrified young man behind the gas station counter. Wet, dishevelled, and really, really annoyed, I squelched my way towards him. A ghastly hush fell over those inside, unable as they were to look away from the wreckage of me. Undaunted,

I haughtily informed the boy that the car wash had experienced a malfunction, and that perhaps someone should have a look. Duty done, I turned and, dripping and squelching, made my way out the door and into my car.

Time has passed. There have been other car washes and other cars. The lessons learned that day remain, however: Firstly, automatic car washes are dangerous places and should be avoided at all costs. Look for manual ones instead or, better still, make someone else wash the car. Secondly, if you must brave an automated car wash, *stay inside the car no matter what happens.* Finally, remember that you are always in control no matter what the car wash tells you. Don't be taken in by the friendly invitation to relax. Remain vigilant at all times and, should you find yourself marooned in the middle of the car washing process, put your car in gear and get the hell out!

THE END OF THE WORLD IN 3 PARTS

The first time the world ended I was six or seven and a local religious group announced that the world would end at midnight that day. I excitedly told the adults around me, thinking that maybe a special supper, at least, would be in order. No one seemed to care. I had to go to school; people did what they usually did and got on with their daily lives. I went to sleep tentatively that night, waiting for something called "The Rapture." Morning came and the world, my world, was just the same as the day before. Not an end in sight.

The next time the world ended I was in Grade 3 and the US president, President Kennedy, was assassinated. Surely any time now the Soviet Union would launch bombs to end my world. But, having survived the Rapture event, I was a little wiser and held on to some hope that while the world might change, we would survive. I was right.

Now, much, much older I watch as the world struggles through COVID-19, conspiracy theories, global recession, and anarchy, and think: DARN IT ALL, WE ARE JUST GOING TO HAVE TO LIVE THROUGH THIS!

DELUSIONS OF GRANDEUR

This will sound pretentious, I know, but I really think that we need a butler to help us move between our various homes. Let me explain. Our home base is a condo near to our daughter and granddaughters in a midsize city in Alberta, Canada. That is the address we use when responding to the question "Where do you live?" That is not true, though. We spend April through September at our house on a lake in a neighbouring province and winters at our place in Quintana Roo, Mexico. How we ended up with all these bits of real estate is a mystery as we are not wealthy, just impetuous and incredibly lucky—being in the right place at the right time sort of thing. Each of our homes has furniture, linens, a fully stocked kitchen, and so on. We keep climate-appropriate clothing at each place. Even with all of that, it feels like we are constantly opening or closing residences. This requires some effort, particularly at the lake house, because we turn off the electricity and the water and bring in all the outdoor stuff.

Hence our need for a butler. In my daydreams, this would be a quiet, elegant fellow, somewhat older than us. We would call him by his last name of course, something like Harris or Jones. Harris/ Jones would precede us to each location to turn on utilities, stock the refrigerator, and oversee cleaning. While we are in residence, he would manage our calendar (because our iPad and iPhone calendar sucks and keeps changing the time zone, so we never know the actual date of anything), do the grocery shopping, and clean the car or the truck, depending upon where we are. It would be great if he would do a little light yard work too but perhaps that is beyond the usual scope of "butlering."

Come to think of it, we may need a maid to do the cleaning that Harris/Jones would oversee. The maid could stay behind to close the place we are leaving, while Harris/Jones would open the next. As we don't have any fireplaces that need to be tended or cleaned, maybe the maid could do the gardening.

Wow—this is going to be great! While we are at it, how about a part-time cook? We can handle breakfast and lunch, but dinner is starting to be a hassle. It interferes with leisurely drinks beforehand. Yeah, I think that a part-time cook is a definite must.

Hmm. Exactly where are we going to keep our future staff? I suppose they will need somewhere to sleep and a separate bathroom. None of our homes has that kind of space. Maybe we will rent separate quarters for them but then that is going to be pricey. Speaking of which, flying Harris/Jones, a maid, and a part-time cook between locations is going to be expensive, and I suppose they will expect to be paid.

Just talked to my financial advisor a.k.a. husband. He says that we cannot afford any staff and that, if I don't stop spending money on my delusions of grandeur, one of the houses may have to go. Darn, I was really starting to like Harris/Jones too.

WEDNESDAY NIGHT BINGO

It doesn't take much. The smell of old wooden floors oiled not waxed or sunscreen on hot bodies. The buttery, salty smell of popcorn or the sight of children sitting absolutely still in anticipation. Any one or all of these will flood me with memories of Wednesday Night Bingo at the lake.

Summer at Ma-Me-O Beach had a rhythm of its own. For kids, it was made of long, hot days of playing: playing in the sand, playing in the water, playing with each other. They were free to come and go between houses or explore the shoreline. Everyone knew who belonged where. Even family dogs could roam around without calls to the pound. By late afternoon, kids and dogs usually drifted to their homes, sticky with sand and sleepy from playing all day in the sun. After supper, families might go out for ice cream or visit neighbours, have one last swim before bed. Unless it was Wednesday. Wednesday nights belonged to Bingo at the community hall.

The community hall sat right beside the playground. It was where dances were held on occasional Friday nights; it was the home of the Farmers' Market on Sundays, and on rainy days it could be full of lake kids working on crafts. There was a stage, a big kitchen, and bathrooms. The hall belonged to no one in particular and everyone in general. It was where our beach community came together, and it felt like home.

On Wednesday nights, the hall was full of long plastic tables and chairs. Bingo cards were sold at the door: one for twenty-five cents, five for a dollar. Originally made from sturdy cardboard with little sliding doors for each square, long use left them grease stained and mostly without sliders. People used all sorts of things to cover up numbers: coins, random paper, even rocks. The caller sat on the stage behind a table holding the Bingo Ball Cage and a huge tray where each ball would be placed after it had been called. There were cash prizes for each round, the amount determined by how many cards had been sold that night. There was an ancient machine that churned out free popcorn. By the end of the night popcorn littered the floor and crunched under foot.

Everyone came. Families with younger children, of course, but seniors and teenagers and people on their own. There were babies on laps and exhausted toddlers asleep on blankets on the floor. This was important, a Ma-Me-O Beach ritual through which kids learned to shout "Clickety-Click" in response to "B-66" or "And after" to "B-4." No one was too cool to shout along. This was our game, our hall, our beach.

As a game was called and the number of Bingo balls on the rack grew, the tension in the hall mounted. Just one more number . . . When it finally came, the shout of "BINGO!" was almost a relief. The prize money, up to ten dollars, was handed to the winner once the Bingo had been verified by the caller. A win confirmed that you had what it took to play the game, that you were lucky and might be again.

As summer moved from July into August, the nights came earlier, and it was quite often dark by the time the last game had been called and the last prize money awarded. Parents holding sleeping children escaped clean-up duty. The rest of us, teenagers included, were expected to sweep floors and put away tables and chairs. No one minded; it was just how it was.

I miss Wednesday Night Bingo. Not just the fun but the current of connectedness that built between participants. *This is us,* it said to everyone who played the game. *This is who we are and what we do on Wednesday nights.* We got to know each other as we swept the floors or handed out popcorn or took a turn holding a sleeping child. And in the knowing came trust and an awareness that we could rely on one another if we had to.

It occurs to me that the world needs more Bingo nights where all you need is twenty-five cents and a willingness to shout "Clickety-Click" to belong. If there is still Bingo in Ma-Me-O next Wednesday night, I am going to go.

HOW TO BUY A HAMMOCK: TRAVELS WITH JUDY PART 1

Years ago, my husband and I took our kids on a camping trip to Mexico. Just saying that gives me shudders, even now, as 1) we are not campers, and 2) this was to be done in the wilds of the Yucatán Peninsula.

This trip began as a rescue mission. My best friend, her husband, and their four kids had left on an extended trip to camp in the wilds of Yucatán at some place called Black's Beach. I had received a letter from her asking me to *"please, please,* come down," as she was feeling a bit overwhelmed. It took a bit of convincing and more than a little luck, but my husband was a good sport and happened upon some cheap flights to Cancún.

Judy and family met us at the airport. We were all going to stay in Cancún for the first week or so, us staying in an air-conditioned hotel by night (bliss) and going on amazing trips during the day courtesy of Judy and Steve's van. We were not their only visitors. Steve's niece and nephew plus their friend had just arrived. That meant that there were often fourteen of us crowded into the van: their family of six, our family of five, and the three others. By taking out a few rows of seats this was doable. Little kids sat on the floor or on laps. Coolers full of ice and cold drinks did double duty as seats. It was entirely in keeping with the adventure we were on to travel this way, and no one complained—at least not about the mode of travel. We did complain, and a lot, about the heat. Transitioning from Canada in March to the Yucatán in March is not for the faint of heart.

We went to amazing and sometimes out of the way places on those road trips. My favourite was our trip to a federal jail to buy hammocks. In Mexico, at that time and in that place, prisoners had to either earn money to buy food and other necessities or rely on their family to supply them. A specialty of the inmates, apparently, was making hammocks by hand to sell in local markets.

As I remember it, the jail was in quite a barren area along a highway somewhere. It was single storied, with a flat roof. Armed guards stood at the door. Our kids—all of them—thought they were awesome and the guards, in turn, were charmed by our seven blonde Canadian kids. The adults were allowed to go through to an inner courtyard, but the kids had to remain outside in the care of their new, albeit armed, playmates.

The courtyard was barren, hot and empty. Standing with more armed guards at our side, we waited as inmates entered the courtyard holding out hammocks, their eyes beseeching us to buy. I remember looking aghast at my husband as he *bargained* with one guy to get the price lowered. *Really, James?* At one point, a guard tapped him on the shoulder and gestured for him to move. He pointed to the flat roof above us, now occupied by guards with rifles pointed down at the inmates. James had inadvertently gotten in the line of fire. This was unlike any other shopping experience I had ever had or could have even imagined.

We selected our seller and our hammock, trying to ignore the eyes of the other inmates. Out of the courtyard, out of the jail, and back to the van, collecting our kids along the way. We all waved goodbye to their new friends, the prison guards.

Years later, we still have that hammock at our lake house. Our kids and grandkids love to lie in it, swaying gently in the sun. I doubt that our kids remember how it came to be ours. But I do.

IS THIS YOUR SWEAT OR MINE?
TRAVELS WITH JUDY PART 2

As explained in "How to Buy a Hammock: Travels with Judy Part 1," our family of five joined their family of six on a trip to the Yucatán. After spending the first week in Cancún, it was time to head to the beach where our friends had been camping for the last several months. Black's Beach, they called it, after the Mayan fisherman who, with his wife and kids, looked after the oceanfront property.

The journey to the beach was arduous. About five hours south of Cancún, the main highway took you only part of the way. Once you turned off and went east towards the ocean, the roads were gravel and full of potholes. Navigating around them added what felt like hours to the journey in a crowded van on a hot day. There were fourteen of us to be driven to the beach. I decided to take the three oldest girls and go by air-conditioned bus to Chetumal, a small city not too far from our beach destination. I claimed this act as being necessary to cut down numbers in the van, thus improving the lot of all. Frankly, I was delighted to take our girls and travel in comfort. While the others endured the more cramped and hot van ride, we had a night out in Chetumal. We resumed our journey the next day in a much less crowded van and finally arrived at the beach.

Black's Beach was glorious, fronted by the turquoise waters of the Caribbean and flanked by jungle. It felt like we had been washed ashore into a bit of paradise. There was an open-air kitchen ruled over by Black's wife, Emparro, an outhouse, and a wood-framed house with bunks and hammocks for sleeping. We set up our tent alongside those of our friends and settled in.

True to form I was overly organized and overly concerned with things that didn't matter. Like trying to keep dust out of a tent pitched on sand. I don't really remember swimming in the ocean, although we must have, or taking walks along the beach, though I am sure we did that too. Moments and experiences jumbled together into a single sensation of sun, heat, jungle, and a crazy rooster that crowed all night long.

One vision, though, completely captivated me: Emparro in her kitchen. The kitchen itself was fascinating. It had a thatched roof with supporting poles but was otherwise open to the elements. Oddly, there was a set of painted wooden cupboards on one side and a modern kitchen table and chairs on the other. Emparro cooked on a wood burning stove made from cement blocks with a flat piece of metal on top. Like a true virtuoso, she manipulated driftwood and coals to get the heat she wanted and then got to work. She cooked freshly caught fish in the coals and fried handmade tortillas on the grill on top. Her food smelled and tasted so good. Best of all, though, were the chickens who occupied their own corner of the kitchen. They not only provided a steady supply of eggs, but their chicks also made post meal clean-up a snap. Emparro would scoop up a handful of chicks after a meal, deposit them on the table, and any crumbs or spills were promptly dealt with.

The time came for all of us, all fourteen of us, to leave the beach and begin our respective journeys home. Unlike our day trips, all the seats had to be put back into the van and all our luggage packed. We needed a plan. Clearly, it would be best if some of us could find an alternate way to Chetumal. There was a bus of sorts that one could catch not far from where we had been camping. The thing was that it came and went on its own peculiar schedule. Trusting local folklore, we identified the day on which the bus was most likely to pass by. That became D-Day. The plan was to send our three oldest girls plus their luggage on the bus leaving only eleven to fit in the van. As added security, we would follow the bus into Chetumal.

D-Day came, and the girls were deposited at the site where the bus was most likely to stop if it indeed came at all. The rest of us crammed in the van, every possible spot for passengers and luggage used. Our seven-year-old lay on top of luggage in the back rear window. Judy's son luckily fit into a huge urn, also in the rear, that they were bringing back to Canada. Adults sat on top of luggage; kids sat on top of adults. There were four of us, including me, in the front. It was a beautiful day if you could spend it in the breeze off the ocean, but in a crowded van it was hell.

We waited in the van by the bus stop—a haphazard lean-to on the side of the jungle—until the bus came. It looked like an old school bus that had seen better days, with bench seats and an odd sort of window situation. If you wanted a window, you simply picked one up off the floor and held it up against the open frame. Our girls bravely boarded, and we were off. Jam-packed as the van was, it rode low over the rough roads. Hitting potholes was an agonizing experience for everyone sitting on luggage. About fifteen minutes down the gravel road, the bus pulled over and stopped. We pulled over too and waited for an explanation. The bus, it turned out, had broken down and everyone had to get off to make their own way either back home or on to Chetumal. The three girls and their luggage now had to be added to the van contingent. We did it but just how escapes me. Now there was fourteen people plus luggage in a van built for seven (without luggage) at most.

If we were riding low before, we barely cleared the road now. People were so tightly packed together that movement was not possible. Everyone was hot and sweating profusely, not knowing exactly if it was their own sweat or their neighbour's that trickled down arms and legs. We became slightly giddy, perhaps hysterical, after a while. Everything was funny and we laughed uproariously as we crunched over gravel and lurched over ruts and potholes.

Eventually we made it to the paved highway and then forty minutes later to Chetumal. As we pulled into the hotel parking, I breathed a sigh of relief. Journey over. We had made it. Overcrowded vehicles were not uncommon—it was not unusual, for example, to see an entire family of four riding a scooter. That said, it must have been some sight to watch fourteen people, clearly tourists, unstick themselves and lurch out of the van.

Our family was staying at the hotel for a night and then taking an *air conditioned and reliable* bus to Cancún and our flight home. Judy and Steve and their kids continued their drive across Mexico and the United States, back to Canada.

Over the years, the tale of The Van Ride has acquired an almost mythical status amongst those who experienced it, and those we tell it to. Like many adventures, the retelling is way more fun than the actual journey but, like true survivors, we are quite proud of ourselves for having come through it.

CPSIA information can be obtained
at www.ICGtesting.com
Printed in the USA
BVHW040535030522
635440BV00008B/185/J

9 781039 135345